A PROMISE Kept

Spiritual Insights for Family Caregivers

BONITA BANDARIES

A Promise Kept

Copyright © 2021 by Bonita Bandaries. All rights reserved.

Photographs by Bonita Bandaries

No part of this publication may be reproduced, stored in a retrieval system or transmitted in any way by any means, electronic, mechanical, photocopy, recording or otherwise without the prior permission of the author except as provided by USA copyright law.

The opinions expressed by the author are not necessarily those of URLink Print and Media.

Scripture quotations marked "MSG" are taken from The Message. Copyright 1993, 1994, 1995, 1996, 2000, 2001, 2002. Used by permission of NavPress Publishing Group.

Scripture quotations marked "NIV" are taken from The Holy Bible, New International Version. Copyright 1973, 1974, 1984 by Biblica. Used by permission of Zondervan Publishing House. All rights reserved.

Scripture quotations marked "NCV" are taken from The Holy Bible, New Century Version. Copyright 1987, 1988, 1991 by Word Publishing, Dallas, Texas 75039. Used by permission.

Scripture quotations marked "NKJV" are taken from The New King James Version of the Bible. Copyright 1979, 1980, 1982, 1984 by Thomas Nelson, Inc. Publishers. Used by permission.

"Television Credits"

The Believer's Voice of Victory." Kenneth Copeland Ministries. Fort Worth, TX, viewed on cable channels.

"The 700 Club." The Christian Broadcasting Network, Inc. Virginia Beach, VA, 24-Hour Prayer Line: 800.700.7000.

1603 Capitol Ave., Suite 310 Cheyenne, Wyoming USA 82001
1-888-980-6523 | admin@urlinkpublishing.com

URLink Print and Media is committed to excellence in the publishing industry.

Book design copyright © 2021 by URLink Print and Media. All rights reserved.

Published in the United States of America

Library of Congress Control Number: 2021920729
ISBN 978-1-64753-996-2 (Paperback)
ISBN 978-1-64753-997-9 (Digital)

29.09.21

Given to: _____

From: _____

Date: _____

"Whoever refreshes others will be refreshed."
Proverbs 11:25 NIV

Dedication

In loving memory of my mother,
Eunice Powell Montgomery

"I have loved you
with an
Everlasting Love."
Jeremiah 31:3 KJV

Acknowledgments

Caregiving experiences impact you deeply and will likely stay with you for life. Once the season of caregiving is over, caregivers face the challenge of life "after caregiving." I gratefully acknowledge family, friends, church, and medical staff who made a difference in caring for my mother during the last decade of her life.

Caregivers have big hearts and recognize the need to make life better for others. Many former caregivers transfer their commitment of care and compassion to the community. They dedicate time, talents, or money through involvement with local issues and organizations. For me, this phase of life opened doors to new friends, challenges, and opportunities to share caregiving spiritual insights and inspiration.

I am grateful:
- for local publishers who printed my thoughts about honoring parents and caring for them.
- for invitations to speak to support groups.
- for opportunities to share information at senior health fairs, expos and various events.

I am grateful to former caregivers who share memories with me. I am especially grateful for God's direction to inspire new caregivers and encourage them.

"Encourage one another daily." Jeremiah 31:25 NCV

Preface

A Promise Kept, Spiritual Insights for Family Caregivers was written to encourage caregivers, particularly those who are caring for aging parents. It is your "self-help" for managing the numerous responsibilities of care while still maintaining a normal life. Even with support from family, friends, medical professionals, support groups, websites, and other sources, caregiving can become exhausting, depressing and stressful. How will you overcome these obstacles? Who will care for the caregiver?

My book focuses on a promise I made to Mother, that being to care for her at home and not in a nursing facility. This is not a commentary against nursing homes for they fulfill a need for many families. Situations are different and each family must make decisions for the best care of the their loved one. Aging, physical disabilities or long-term care coupled with the situation of the likely caregiver are just a few factors to consider.

While caring for my mother, I found confidence, encouragement and hope to guide me through the caregiving experience. Loving your family and choosing to provide care does not make you immune to the effects of that care physically and emotionally.

God provides tools to meet challenges and care for us through scriptures. Jesus is our caregiver when we depend on Him for our cares. Caregiving situations can change from one moment to the next but God will provide for our needs when we ask Him and believe. This I did by reading scriptures, hearing the word taught, and sharing devotionals with Mother. I later learned that research supports spirituality and says it makes caregiving easier and gives you peace after caregiving.

A Promise Kept, Spiritual Insights for Family Caregivers is my story of caregiving relying on God's Promises to support the process of working with medical staff and meeting other needs. I encourage family caregivers by sharing information at health fairs, book signings, and especially during November, National Family Caregivers Month when I coordinate an event to recognize family caregivers in my community.

I recommend *A Promise Kept, Spiritual Insights for Family Caregivers*:
- to all who are in the decision phase of caring for elderly parents.
- to all family caregivers, especially those who are new to the role.
- to friends and family for understanding family caregivers.

I pray this book will bless caregivers with inspiration from God's Promises revealed in the Bible.

God's Promises to Care for Caregivers

I will provide for their needs before they ask, and I will help them while they are still asking for help.
Isaiah 65:24 NCV

So, I tell you, ask, and God will give to you. Search, and you will find. Knock, and the door will open.
Luke 11:9 NCV

And, if you ask for anything in my name, I will do it for you so that the Father's glory will be shown through the son. If you ask me for anything in my name, I will do it.
John 14:13-14 NCV

God speaks to us through his Word, dreams, visions, and sometimes in an audible voice.

I was challenged by the words of Isaiah 30:8 NIV
"Go now, write it on a tablet for them, inscribe it on a scroll, that for the days to come it may be an everlasting witness."

After Mother's passing, I collected posted notes and assorted scraps of paper with hastily written verses to read as I went about my daily tasks or paused to rest. Reflecting on these, a book of encouragement began to form in my mind.

One morning as I was searching for a title, muttering and asking God to give me a title, He did!

I heard the words ***A Promise Kept*** softly spoken. I must admit that I have always been skeptical of people who say they hear God speak. But looking around and seeing no one, standing in reverent silence, I was certain I was experiencing a rare moment to be treasured, one which has given me direction for a decade of *A Promise Kept*.

Contents

Dedication 7
Acknowledgments 9
Preface 11
God's Promises to Care for Caregivers 13
Introduction 17
Take Care of Your Mother 19
    The Promise 23
    The Decision 25
    A Duty of Children 27
    Honor 28
    Mother's Diagnosis 29
    Wisdom 30
    Believing God...31
Strategies and Scriptures for Caregiver Self-Care....35
    Trust 37
    I Trust You, Lord... 38
    Trust Versus Anxiety 39
    Prayer 40
    How May I Pray for You? 41
    Petition 42
    Seek The Lord..43
    Healing 45
    The God of Healing 46
    Mother's Healings 47
    Faith 48
    Praise 49
    Honoring God 50

    Courage and Strength 51
    Not By My Might..52
    Perseverance..53
    Never Tire of Doing Good... 54
    Worry 56
    Fear...57
    Rest...58
    Blessed Sleep... 60
    Peace 61
    Love 63
    Everlasting Love 64
    Joy.. 65
    Take Heart... 66
    Thanks 68
    A Grateful Heart 69
Conclusion 71
Refresh Your Heart: The 5 R's for Caregivers 73
About the Author..75
Bonita's Books 77

Introduction

A Decade of A Promise Kept

Family caregivers are people like you and me. Some are seniors caring for spouses or aging parents while others may care for disabled family members, children, siblings, or friends. Sometimes they live in the same house with you while others live in their own homes. Many caregivers have families and may still work outside the home.

A Promise Kept, Spiritual Insights for Family Caregivers addresses caregiving using wisdom from God's word to guide that care. Acknowledging God's guidance does not exclude medical treatment, physicians, and technology. There are too many variables associated with them to discuss in this book which is to give you direction and confidence in making decisions using spiritual wisdom. Praying and meditating using God's Word needs to be your first priority. It is essential in this season of caring for ill loved ones.

Family and friends may not understand your commitment to care for a loved one and all that may include. Be prepared for stressful times when:

- Family members say they will help but don't.
- Friends who don't understand when you can't attend social events.
- You indulge in bouts of feeling sorry for yourself for having little or no personal time.

The emotional stress of caregiving often leads to health issues for the one giving care. Self-care is important in order to give care. Self-care means taking time for yourself, giving your mind and body rest. Let your meditation and prayer be your guide for confidence, clarity, and compassion in your role of caregiving. *A Promise Kept, Spiritual Insights for Family Caregivers* cites some scriptures I used for the morning, during the day, and in the evening.

God is faithful to provide wisdom and strength making caregiving more than possible. Let the scriptures fill your mind and heart. Find scriptures and promises that speak to you. Read them, reread them, and commit them to memory.

I am not saying the caregiving journey will always be easy and trouble-free but God's promises revealed in the scriptures are as relevant today as when first given hundreds of centuries ago. They have spanned the decades of time and are everlasting.

Take Care of Your Mother

"Take care of your mother," Dad said in his last days before a fast-moving cancer took his life.

These words spoken to my brother, sister and me by my dad from his hospital bed were heartbreaking and almost unbearable to hear. In their last years together, Dad accepted more responsibility of household chores, shopping, and maintaining tasks typically done by Mother. Her arthritis became more painful and debilitating making visits to doctors and the pain clinic more frequent.

At the time of Dad's death, Mother was no longer driving, used a cane and wheelchair and seldom left home. The arthritis along with other medical issues restricted her activities making her dependent on my dad for assistance. Though she was an excellent cook and loved the task, Mother could only microwave dishes already prepared. With help from family on weekends, home health during the week and a weekly housekeeper, my parents maintained a quality of life until Dad was stricken with cancer.

All the family enjoyed visiting my parents at their retirement home on a lake in rural East Texas. Dad loved fishing from his pier and frying fish for everyone. We were amused at his stories of learning to make cornbread, make breakfast and even clean the kitchen. This was from a man who had never prepared so much as a sandwich. Dad's role had always been taking care of the outside of the home while Mother cared for the inside. At the time no one thought of Dad as a "caregiver" but realized that he was terrific at the role reversal. Seeing them together as Dad drove Mother to appointments, the image was that of an elderly couple taking care of each other.

After Dad's passing, Mother refused to consider leaving her home. Wanting to honor her wishes, we attempted to care for her from a distance. It became my role as the oldest and unencumbered by family to continue Dad's tasks. Traveling to and from another town and periodic stayovers were not enough. Finances prohibited live-in caregivers and part-time help was difficult to find. Home health nurses were on call and an aide visited for an hour twice a week. Since the neighbors were also elderly or worked, there was no one to monitor her care. Still, Mother insisted she was able to stay alone and wanting her to make the decision to leave her home, we hesitated too long insisting that she do so.

Mother's health began deteriorating rapidly. She could not manipulate her electric wheelchair effectively, hitting doors and furniture, and turning over in her chair several times. Eventually, she fell using her cane and fractured a hip.

Her stay in a rehabilitation facility, followed by home therapists was not enough to completely restore her mobility. A few months later, Mother's stay at her home ended when she fell on both knees attempting to get into her wheelchair.

The Promise

As far back as I can remember, Mother would say to her children, "Please, never put me in a nursing home!" It's easy to agree to requests made by your mother when that request seems a long way off.

My sister sometimes laughs remembering this frequent statement from Mother whose opinion was based on observations of several relatives who spent their last years in nursing homes. Mother was a conscientious and compassionate caregiver whenever she was called upon to do so. She believed family should care for aging or ill loved ones at home. Growing up we often had grandparents or other relatives stay with us to recover from an illness. No one ever thought caring for family as a job but just what families did.

Mother would no longer be able to stay in her home seventy-five miles away and in a rural setting. Though she did not want to live with me, Mother knew that it was the only alternative to a nursing home. I had often asked Mother to live with me and had even moved from my two-story home to one more accommodating for handicapped needs. I never thought that she would have no mobility and I wasn't sure I was prepared to become a round-the-clock caregiver.

In addition to physical conditions, Mother's controlling temperament made it difficult to get along with her. In her mind, she was having difficulty accepting the reality that she could not make all decisions. My brother knowing this trait felt it would be best for her to go to a nursing facility. My sister wanted to meet Mother's request but was also concerned about her getting quality care at home. Of course, friends and other family members offered their advice which was divided.

Ultimately, the decision would be mine since it would be with me that she would need to live. A major life change was about to me made which would affect not only Mother but my life and that of my siblings who would be expected to help. I wanted to do what was best for Mother's care and at the same time keep a promise but would keeping that promise deny her better health care?

I needed reassurance and confidence about making the right decision. The answer is always. "Pray about it."

The Decision

Wise decisions call for prayer and trust to receive God's direction. My experiences had taught me that when something is meant to be, all areas come into place and there is peace about the issue. During Mother's initial hospital stay, I prayed a lot and tried to analyze all possible options. One disturbing factor was a comment from a doctor who said that most elderly people who cannot walk and must stay in bed or chairs die within eighteen months from infections or pneumonia. This increased my seeking God's guidance, and confidence to make the right decision.

When children need to become caregivers, there likely has not been adequate planning, if any, to prepare for this life-changing event. This was true for me even though I had been helpful in so many ways to my parents. But whether there has been advance planning or not, there are many questions to be answered. Leaving their home and role reversals of parents and children foster emotional issues on both sides of the spectrum.

Should I care for my Mother in my home or seek an alternative? This question was not easily answered as stated in "The Promise." Wanting to honor Mother's request was not easy considering her medical issues. At the top of the list of concerns was whether I could do this since I had no experience in caring for anyone with mobility issues and serious health needs. Caring for her in my home would require a different lifestyle for me, too.

The decision to bring Mother to my home was grounded in believing the scripture "the Lord would make me wise and show me where to go." God's Word, her desire, and medical advice were the criteria. Actually, the decision was made for me by Mother and her doctor or rather, confirmed my decision.

Mother and her pulmonologist (have I told you that Mother had COPD?) bonded I think because she reminded him of his mother who was the same age. He told Mother he visited his mother each day before making daily rounds; his credibility reached new heights in her eyes. His interest in her well-being was to become a catalyst in Mother's recovery from numerous hospital stays to come.

One afternoon I arrived at the rehabilitation hospital to learn that the two of them had ordered a hospital bed for my home and arranged home health staff to visit! Though he was her pulmonologist, he became Mother's primary care doctor directing home health which was to be an invaluable asset to her care.

Would you say this was God answering my prayers for guidance? Seemed so to me!

A Duty of Children

Honor your father and your mother, as the LORD your God has commanded you that your days may be long, and that it may be well with you in the land which the Lord your God is giving you.
Deuteronomy 5:16 NKJV

Children, obey your parents in the Lord, for this is right. "Honor your father and mother," the first commandment with promise: "that it may be well with you and you may live long on the earth."
Ephesians 6:1-3 NKJV

Honor your father and your mother . . .
Matthew 19:19 NKJV

Children, obey your parents in all things, for this is well pleasing to the Lord.
Colossians 3:20 NKJV

But if any widow has children or grandchildren, let them first learn to show piety at home and "to repay their parents; for this is good and acceptable before God.
1 Timothy 5:4 NKJV

God promises us that if we follow the commandment to honor our parents, "it will be well with us and may have long life on the earth."
Ephesians 6:1-3 NKJV

Honor

The Bible talks a lot about family and clearly commands children to honor their parents. The commandment given by God is the first commandment with promise—that children's days may be long.

Respecting my parents had always been easy and done without question. Growing up in church I was taught to live by this commandment. As an adult, interacting with my parents, respect came easy. No event until now had caused so much inner turmoil especially when it involved such a major life change for all the family.

How will this new obligation affect me and the rest of the family? Respecting one's wishes should be in line with what is in the best interest of the person needing care. Can the physical, medical, and emotional needs be met in the home? What is the physical, emotional, and financial condition of the caregiver?

I lived alone and had room to accommodate all the medical equipment needed. Home health was available, specialists could do home visits, and medical facilities were nearby.

Mother's Diagnosis

Mother was an 82-year-old lady who had severe arthritis in her knees before she fell; she likely would never walk again. She would be coming from the rehab hospital with casts on both broken legs and having a serious wound on her backside which must be treated daily by wound care specialists. Complicating matters would be her COPD, chronic obstructive pulmonary disease, and other disorders such as diverticulitis.

Along with the physical concerns was Mother's reluctance towards living with me. She knew she was welcome to my home but had declined to do this for several years. The change would be difficult, create conflict and life for both of us would change. Although many well-meaning people advised against becoming my mother's full-time caregiver, I chose to fulfill a promise to Mother and honor God's commandment.

Wisdom

The LORD says, I will make you wise and show you where to go. I will guide you and watch over you."
Psalm 31:8 NCV

Trust the LORD with all your heart, and don't depend on your own understanding.
Remember the LORD in all you do, and He will give you success.
Don't depend on your own wisdom. Respect the LORD and refuse to do wrong.
Proverbs 3:5-7 NCV

For the LORD gives wisdom;
From His mouth come knowledge and understanding.
Proverbs 2:6 NKJV

How did these scriptures help me when I needed wisdom?

I would read the verse and speak to the Lord as, *"Lord, you said if I lack wisdom, ask you and you will give it to me liberally. I am asking expecting to receive it and I thank you for it."* James 1:5 KJV

Positive statements reframe the situation from uncertainty to confidence and clarity to make decisions. I learned to rely on God's direction through the scriptures.

Believing God

◆

Believing that *"the Lord would make me wise and show me where to go,"* I brought Mother to live with me. Like most elderly, sick patients, she had difficulty adjusting to changes in her life. She met them with resistance often berating me with angry words when I followed doctor's orders and not hers. *"You don't know anything! You're just a teacher,"* she would frequently blurt out meaning I did not know about medicines.

I was reminded of Jesus words in Mark 6:4 when He said,

> "A *prophet is not without honor except in his own country, among his own relatives, and in his own house."*

I certainly was not a prophet and not perfect. Her taunting comments did anger me making it essential to control my own emotions. I needed advice and counseling to keep from being overwhelmed since this was more involved than my role as a school counselor so God became my counselor.

Trusting God for wisdom must be done daily over many details such as routines of personal care, food, medicines, finding appropriate help if needed, scheduling home providers, when the patient needs more specific medical assistance, and finances. Because situations can change within a day and more often in the night, wisdom is needed.

The caregiver can feel so lonely and alone caring for a patient in the night when changes can occur suddenly. An example is that of my mother whose lungs were very diminished. In fact, her lungs were more critical than having no mobility. It was not easy to determine if her breathing was labored indicating onset of pneumonia. Mother frequently developed respiratory infections and had to be treated in and out of the hospital. Because the Lord always answered my prayer for wisdom, I listened for His promptings of spiritual advice.

A wonderful prayer that the Lord answered was for Mother to keep a sound mind. There were times when medicine affected her memory but this occurred after periods of illness requiring strong antibiotics. Being able to watch Christian ministry and read the Bible together was an antidote for rough cycles of stress. She had a strong faith in spite of oppression.

As often as Mother felt strong enough, we spent time outside meditating in the garden. This was healthy for Mother, but respite for me. Meditation, quietly enjoying nature in any setting is a self-care strategy for caregivers. Being in the beauty of God's creation, feeling His presence refreshes and renews the spirit.

My Meditation

Of Him Shall Be Sweet;
I Will Be Glad In The Lord.

Psalm 104:34 KJV

Strategies and Scriptures for Caregiver Self-Care

Trust

Trust God from the bottom of your heart;
Don't try to figure out everything on your own.
Listen for God's voice in everything you do,
Everywhere you go;
He's the one who will keep you on track.
Proverbs 3: 5-6 MSG

God is our refuge and strength,
A very present help in trouble.
Psalm 46:1 NKJV

Give all your worries to him because He cares for you.
1 Peter 5:7 NCV

Blessed is the man who makes the Lord his trust.
Psalm 40:4 NIV

Those who trust in the LORD are like Mount Zion,
Which cannot be shaken but endures forever.
Psalm 125:1 NIV

I Trust You, Lord

Scriptures are prescriptions for caregivers! A caregiver must trust that he/she will be alert, observant, giving their loved one timely and appropriate care as needed. I found it necessary to quote passages often to remind myself that God was my strength and not to be afraid of knowing when to seek medical advice about concerns. No question is too trivial to ask when in doubt. I was thankful for quick responses from Mother's doctor and home health nurses who were always on call.

Worries, concerns take many forms according to the mental and physical condition of the loved one. I worried that I would not hear Mother in the night calling for help. One example concerned Mother getting out of bed at night not remembering that she could not stand on her feet. She did not like having a hospital bed nor having to sleep in it. Sometimes I would wake to the sound of her shaking the bars trying to get out; she did dislodge them several times and fell to the floor.

Coping with emotional stress of roles reversing to a child caring for parent requires an act of will. Anxiety, frustration, hurt or angry feelings are common reactions when caring for parents who are likely experiencing them too. I trusted God to keep emotions in check and guide my reactions to Mother's behavior. This was not always easy for me!

Trust Versus Anxiety

Speaking positive reactions fosters trust instead of anxiety.

Lord, I give you my worries and cares!

Spoken aloud, but softly to myself, this changed the atmosphere from chaotic to peaceful. Sometimes I spoke louder to engage Mother which seemed to refocus her anxiety as well as mine.

Learning to rely on God's direction in this new season of life took faith and trust for both of us, for me it was the awesome responsibility of providing care and for Mother it was having faith to relinquish care of herself to a daughter.

How encouraging the scriptures became! To overcome intense emotional outbursts and restore peace and harmony, Mother and I listened to Christian music, watched programs, or prayed aloud together. This was part of our daily routine. I was blessed and thankful that Mother was a Christian and enjoyed worship and devotion.

Prayer

Anyone who is having troubles should pray.
James 5:13 NCV

Pray without ceasing.
Thessalonians 5:17 NKJV

And whatever things you ask in prayer, believing, you will receive.
Matthew 21:22 NKJV

Evening, morning, and noon I cry out in distress, and he hears my voice.
Psalm 55:17 NIV

Don't fret or worry. Instead of worrying, pray. Let petitions and praises shape your worries into prayer, letting God know your concerns. Before you know it a sense of God's wholeness, everything coming together for good, will come and settle you down. It's wonderful what happens when Christ displaces worry at the center of your life.
Philippians 4:6-7 MSG

How May I Pray for You?

The Bible tells us not to worry but pray without ceasing. This should be a reality for the caregivers for there are so many things to pray for: guidance in care, health, healing, peace and numerous other needs. We are told that whatever we need we should ask for believing that it will be granted. This is a blessing! Sometimes we must stand praying without ceasing for lengths of time. Self-talk turns scriptures into statements, a strategy to turn negative thoughts and actions to positive ones.

Mother was an avid viewer of Christian television and several shows in particular which prayed for people's needs. She frequently called the prayer lines requesting prayer. These volunteer prayer partners are wonderful sources of strength. They stand in agreement with you for your needs. Day or night someone is always available to pray with you. Many nights when I was awake caring for Mother, I called prayer lines for her health needs. We saw results!

A miracle was witnessed one night when my sister and I were preparing Mother for the night. She was frightened because of difficulty breathing that evening. Poised to administer her breathing treatment, about to place the mask on her face, a voice was heard from the television. "Someone is fearful about breathing but you are alright." We both stood speechless hearing reassuring words Mother needed!

Petition

―――◆―――

May the LORD fulfill all your petitions.
Psalm 20:5 NKJV

Blessed Be God, who has not turned away my prayer, nor His mercy from me.
Psalm 66:20 NKJV

And if you ask for anything in my name, I will do it for you so that the Father's glory will be shown through the Son. If you ask me for anything in my name, I will do it.
John 14:13-14 NCV

Therefore, I say to you, whatever things you ask when you pray, believe that you receive them, and you will have them.
Mark 11:24 NKJV

Don't fret or worry. Instead of worrying, pray. Let petitions and praises shape your worries into prayer, letting God know your concerns. Before you know it, a sense of God's wholeness, everything coming together for good will come and settle you down. It's wonderful what happens when Christ displaces worry at the center of your life.
Philippians 4:6-7 NCV

Seek The Lord

The Bible is filled with passages telling us to seek the Lord. He cares about our cares. These positive scriptures are inspiring. They give you strength to pursue your routine tasks under stress.

Believing that God heard my requests, I saw many situations resolve because of petitioning Him. No matter what happens, we are asked to keep on praying and asking God for answers, always thanking Him for working in our lives.

Petitions are specific requests made of God on your behalf. There are other specific prayers, for example, thanksgiving.

> *"Seek the LORD and His strength, seek His face evermore! Remember His marvelous works which He has done, His wonders and the judgments of His mouth."*
> Psalm 105: 4-5 KJV

This means that we must spend time with Him recognizing His power. We may have to experience many trials as we stand in faith believing for our requests. Trials come in many forms ranging from sudden medical crisis of your loved one to having to cancel your appointments because the sitter did not arrive on time or maybe not at all. Any number of things can disrupt or alter your schedule. I spent many hours of my day seeking the LORD!

Remember, God gives you strength to do what you might think impossible. Trust Him with your petitions because He hears you.

> *I sought the LORD and He heard me.*
> Psalm 34:4 NKJV

He heard me calling for help when I was dialing 911 at the same time I was administering CPR and putting oxygen on Mother. This medical emergency happened so quickly! One minute I was talking with her as I walked about ten feet across the room for her breathing treatment. The next minute she was already blue and not breathing!

Paramedics arrived just as Mother was beginning to respond. She looked up at them smiling, saying, "You saved my life!" "No ma'am, your daughter did."

The realization of how quickly a crisis can occur is shocking. But God was present to meet Mother's need. Up till this time I had become so focused on praying to hear her at night and not providing care when needed that I had not anticipated a daytime life situation. I recognized that God would not let me down. Humbly I thanked Him for saving my mother's life and using my hands to do what I thought I could never do.

Healing

And the prayer of faith will save the sick, and the Lord will raise him up.
James 5:15 NKJV

Heal me, O LORD, and I shall be healed; save me, and I shall be saved, For You are the one I praise.
Jeremiah 17:14 NIV

Who Himself bore our sins in His own body on the tree, that we having died to our sins, might live for righteousness--by whose stripes you were healed.
1 Peter 2:24 NKJV

O LORD my God, I cried out to You and You healed me.
Psalm 30:2 NKJV

Also, I tell you that if two of you on earth agree about something and pray for it, it will be done for you by my Father in heaven.
Matthew 18:19 NCV

Bless the LORD, O my soul; and all that is within me, bless His holy name!
Bless the LORD, O my soul, and forget not all His benefits;
Who forgives all your iniquities, who heals all your diseases.
Psalm 103:1-3 NKJV

The God of Healing

God encourages us to call upon Him for healing.
Exodus 15:26b NKJV, *"I am the LORD who heals you."*
We must ask God in faith for healing, believe that He is at work, and trust Him for the outcome.

We must not doubt! Jesus in Matthew 21:21 NKJV tells us about speaking to the fig tree:

"I tell you the truth, if you have faith and do not doubt, you will be able to do what I did to this tree and even more. You will be able to say to this mountain, 'Go, fall into the sea.' And if you have faith, it will happen."

Healing ministries use this passage and believe that we must speak to the infirmity, tell it to leave our body, and believe. Countless authors have written books citing scriptures to be spoken for healing. It is believed that scriptures should be spoken aloud and specific requests be made to the healing needed. I used this technique every day to speak healing scriptures for my mother and myself.

Mother's Healings

God did not suddenly make Mother walk again or eliminate her emphysema from fifty years of smoking but He did heal in daily situations such as restoring her breathing to a safe level. He gave doctors wisdom to try different medicines to wipe out pneumonia when she wasn't responding. Her skin was very fragile and delicate making it easy to tear when bumped even slightly. God healed so many daily occurrences too numerous to mention here but were necessary. During these trials, she and I prayed together, believing God for her healing.

Christian television has many programs where this is demonstrated. One of Mother's favorite healing ministries was that of Gloria Copeland who uses the scriptures to teach people to claim their healing. As God's promise of healing is spoken in faith, believe that it has already happened.

We approach God with our petitions and trust for His answers. His healing may include medicine and professional medical help.

During Mother's stay with me, she was hospitalized numerous times. Sometimes serious healing came through doctors. In these times, I trusted God to direct us even when doctors said she would not live through the night!

Faith

So, then faith comes by hearing, and hearing by the word of God.
Romans 10:17 NKJ

For we walk by faith, not by sight.
2 Corinthians 5:7 NKJV

Be brave, be strong. Don't give up. Expect God to be here soon.
Psalm 31:24 MSG

Cast your burden on the LORD, and He shall sustain you; He shall never permit the Righteous to be moved.
Psalm 55:22 NKJV

So Jesus answered and said to them, "Have faith in God. For assuredly, I say to you,
Whoever says to this mountain, 'Be removed and be cast into the sea' and does not
Doubt in his heart, but believes that those things he says will be done, he will have whatever he says.
Mark 11:22-23 NKJV

Praise

I will praise You, O LORD, with my whole heart.
I will tell of all Your marvelous works.
Psalm 9:1 NKJV

Sing to him; sing praises to him, tell about all his miracles.
Be glad that you are his; let those who seek the Lord be happy.
Depend on the Lord and his strength; always go to him for help.
Remember the miracles he has done, his wonders, and his decisions.
1 Chronicles 16: 9-12 NCV

Now therefore, our God, we thank You and praise Your glorious name.
1 Chronicles 29:13 NKJV

Praise the Lord! For it is good to sing praises to our God; For it is pleasant, and praise is beautiful.
Psalm 147:1 NKJV

Praise Him for His mighty acts;
Praise Him according to His excellent greatness!
Psalm 150:2 NKJV

Honoring God

Praise is honoring the LORD, giving Him respect for who He is and what He does. When circumstances are difficult and there is pain and suffering, we still must find those things for which to praise God. Praise Him for His presence and His mercy which is everlasting and new each morning.

Caring for Mother, I praised Him that He gave me the strength to physically attend to her personal needs. She was never able to stand or walk after the fall and had to be lifted and transferred from place to place. Never one to stay in bed, Mother sat in a lift chair placed in the great room where she could interact with all the day's activities.

A small wheel chair made eating in the dining room possible and when her health permitted for sitting on the patio. We thanked God for days that she felt like being taken to church, the beauty shop, or simply enjoying the patio.

I particularly praised God for having happy moments, peaceful days when she talked, laughed, and could enjoy visitors. But no matter how she felt physically, she frequently was seen raising her hand and quoting:

Hebrews 13:5 NKJV *"My LORD will never leave me nor forsake me."*

Courage and Strength

*Be of good courage, and He shall strengthen your heart,
All you who hope in the LORD.*
Psalm 31:24 NKJV

Depend on the LORD and His strength. Always go to him for help.
1 Chronicles 16:11 NCV

He gives strength to those who are tired and more power to those who are weak.
Isaiah 40:29 NCV

God is our refuge and strength, a very present help in trouble.
Psalm 46:1 NKJV

I can do all things through Christ who strengthens me.
Philippians 4:13 NKJV

My grace is enough for you. When you are weak, my power is made perfect in you.
2 Corinthians 12:9 NCV

When days turn into weeks and weeks to months, caregivers need a plan to maintain their physical health as well as their emotional and spiritual health. Ideas can be found in my book, *A Caregiver Tip A Day, Reframing Your Story.*

Not By My Might

As a caregiver, I gave so much of myself that I habitually neglected my own needs and depended on strength from God's promise about His strength. One particular scripture was really my mantra. Philippians 4:13 KJV says,

> "I can do all things through Christ who strengthens me."

When it seemed that I could not put one foot in front of the other, I would say this verse with passion. Particularly during the night when I was called to Mother's bedside, I spoke this verse with fervor because it seemed that my weary body could not move without God's strength.

As I cared for her, a thought always flashed through my mind. "Do all as unto the LORD" and reminded me to be kind, gentle, and try not to show my tiredness. I never wanted Mother to feel that I did not or could not care for her.

I pray that these verses will minister to other caregivers giving them strength and courage to care for their caree with love and understanding when their own bodies are weary and minds are tired.

Perseverance

And let us not grow weary while doing good;
for in due season, we shall reap if we do not lose heart.
Galatians 6:9 NKJV

Praying always with all prayer and supplication in the Spirit, being watchful
To this end with all perseverance and supplication for all the saints.
Ephesians 6:18 NKJV

And only that, but we also glory in tribulations,
Knowing that tribulation produces perseverance and perseverance, character, and character hope.
Romans 5:3-4 NKJV

Watch, stand fast in the faith, be brave, be strong.
1 Corinthians 16:13 NKJV

But you, brothers and sisters, never become tired of doing good.
2 Thessalonians 3:13 NCV

Never Tire of Doing Good

Caregiving can be overwhelming but by keeping our eyes on Jesus, believing in His goodness, the strenuous tasks can be performed. I discovered that I had to acquire humility.

While doing menial, not pleasant tasks, I occasionally had to remind myself that all work is good in God's eyes. He said that we should not grow weary in well-doing but count it all joy when we encounter difficulties and keep praising him for His goodness.

I was always concerned that others caring for Mother might neglect her personal care because it was unpleasant and frequent. I expected her to be treated with respect and dignity. I never expected paid workers or volunteers to do things I did not do myself but I did expect them to be patient and handle my mother with care. I found it vitally important that I pray over all who came into contact with Mother. My desire was that she experience the best quality of life possible.

PEACE

Let Your Heart Not Be Troubled,
Neither Let It Be Afraid.

John 14:27 KJV

Worry

Who of you by worrying can add a single hour to your life?
Since you cannot do this very little thing, why do you worry about the rest?
Luke 12:25 NIV

Therefore, humble yourselves under the mighty hand of God,
That He may exalt you in due time,
Casting all your care upon Him,
For He cares for you.
1 Peter 5:6-7 NKJV

So don't worry about tomorrow, because tomorrow will have its own worries.
Each day has enough trouble of its own.
Matthew 6:34 NCV

So don't worry, because I am with you. Don't be afraid, because I am Your God. I will make you strong and will help you;
I will support you with
My right hand that saves you.
Isaiah 41:10 NCV

Fear

Fear not ..... for I am your God. I will strengthen you. Yes, I will help you. I will uphold you with my righteous right hand.
Isaiah 41:10 NKJV

So, we say with confidence, "The Lord is my helper; I will not be afraid. What can man do to me?"
Hebrews 13:6 NIV

God did not give us a spirit that makes us afraid but a spirit of power and Love and self-control.
2 Timothy 1:7 NCV

Emotions of worry and fear are counter-productive to all God's promises. They take their toll on the caregiver's body.

During the time of caring for Mother, one of my physical examinations indicated that I needed to begin medication for high cholesterol. In response to the physician advising me not to neglect my diet, exercise, and avoid stress, I explained to him what I was experiencing as a caregiver. He reminded me that worry would not add a single hour to Mother's life or mine.

God's Word was my most important prescription but I was violating a cardinal rule of caregiving: Take care of yourself in order to give care. I needed to trust God's promises for rest.

Rest

―――――◆―――――

Come to me, all of you who are tired and have heavy loads, And I will give you rest. Accept my teachings and learn From me, because I am gentle and humble in spirit, and You will find rest for your lives.
Matthew 11:28 NCV

You wake me each morning with the sound of your loving voice, I'll go to sleep each night trusting in you.
Psalm 145:8 MSG

I lay down and slept; I awoke for the LORD sustained me.
Psalm 3:5-6 NKJV

When you lie down, you will not be afraid; Yes, you will lie down and your sleep will be sweet.
Proverbs 3:24 NKJV

The wise counsel God gives when I'm awake Is confirmed by my sleeping heart.
Day and night
I'll stick with God;
I've got a good thing going and I'm not letting go.
Psalm 16:7-8 MSG

I find rest in God,
Only He gives me hope.
Psalm 62:5 NCV

Blessed Sleep

Caregivers tend to suffer from sleep and rest deprivation. I was no exception! Scriptures are soothing for both the caregiver and the patient. Both need to feel God's assurance that He will watch over them through the night.

The mind, body, and soul require rest in order to function effectively. God's Word tells us that He will provide that if we only trust Him to do so. When I became tired from lack of sleep, routine tasks were more difficult to perform. I finally accepted that it was all right for me to rest when Mother rested. I did not have to be busy with tasks every minute.

Lack of focus is a symptom of sleep deprivation. I did not focus as clearly and would ask myself questions like, "Did I give that medication?" I also became more irritable and stressful.

The Lord's Word said He would give us rest so I depended on Him to give me that throughout the day. Knowing what the Word said about rest restored my strength to perform with minimal sleep. David said in Psalm 16:8 MSG,

> *"Day and night I'll stick with God: I've got a good thing going and I'm not letting go."*

Peace

And the peace of God, which transcends all understanding,
Will guard your hearts and your minds in Christ Jesus.
Philippians 4:7 NIV

Peace I leave with you. My peace I give to you;
Not as the world gives do I give to you. Let not
heart be troubled, neither let it be afraid.
John 14:27 NKJV

Peace, peace, to those far and near,"
Says the LORD. "And I will heal them."
Isaiah 57:19 NIV

Now may the Lord of peace give you peace
At all times and in every way. The LORD
Be with all of you.
2 Thessalonians 3:16 NCV

The LORD will give strength to His people;
The LORD will bless His people with peace.
Psalm 29:11 NKJV

My People
Will Live In Peaceful Places
In Safe Homes And
In Calm Places Of Rest.

Isaiah 32:18 NCV

Love

Love the LORD your God and always obey his orders, rules, laws, and commands.
Deuteronomy 11:1 NCV

I will love You, O LORD, my strength.
Psalm 18:1 NKJV

I love the LORD,
Because He has heard my voice and my supplications.
I love those who love me,
those who seek me diligently will find me.
Psalm 116:1-2 NKJV

My children, we should love people not only with words and talk, But by our actions and true caring.
1 John 3:18 NCV

Because He has inclined His ear to me, therefore I will call upon Him as long as I live.
Psalm 116:2 KJV

Everlasting Love

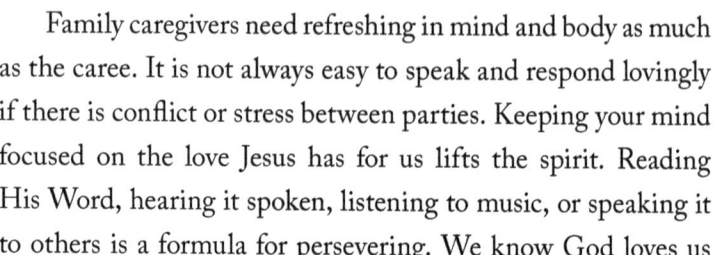

Family caregivers need refreshing in mind and body as much as the caree. It is not always easy to speak and respond lovingly if there is conflict or stress between parties. Keeping your mind focused on the love Jesus has for us lifts the spirit. Reading His Word, hearing it spoken, listening to music, or speaking it to others is a formula for persevering. We know God loves us because He said so and we can do all things, including give and receive love, through Christ who strengthens us.

By keeping Mother in my home, I sometimes struggled with the thought that no amount of love and care was making her happy. She never accepted that my home had become hers. She frequently complained to health care providers that I did not treat her right. They would smile and reassure her that she was well-cared for and had a great nurse. I learned early on not to be embarrassed by such outbursts. I chose to stay focused on God's strength and to continue caring for her with love.

In brief unexpected moments, Mother would speak about her childhood, her family, thoughts, good memories, hurts and disappointments. This was enlightening and made me see her with a new understanding.

Joy

A cheerful disposition is good for your health; Gloom and doom leave you bone-tired.
Proverbs 17:22 MSG

If people please God, God will give them wisdom, knowledge, and joy.
Ecclesiastes 2:26 NCV

I pray that the God who gives hope will fill you with much Joy and peace while you trust in him. Then your hope will overflow by the power of the Holy Spirit.
Romans 15:13 NCV

My brethren, count it all joy when you fall into various trials.
James 1:2 NKJV

These things I have spoken to you, that My joy may remain in you, and that your joy may be full.
John 15:11 NKJV

Be joyful because you have hope.
Romans 12:12 NCV

Take Heart

Knowing and believing in the other promises of God brings hope to persevere, to continue caring for another with love and understanding. Praising God increases one's joy and the opportunity to benefit from His blessings even more. All of the promises work together to strengthen mind and body. The caregiver and the patient are both His children and can take heart in the knowledge of God as revealed in

Psalm 31:15 NIV: *Our times are in His hands.*

The Lord blessed Mother by seeing her through a major surgery which was crucial for life. We were forewarned that her lungs were so weak that she may not get off the ventilator. If she did breathe on her own, she could possibly get pneumonia and may not survive. Neither situation occurred; however, the doctors identified a heart valve which needed replacing. This was not possible so more medications were prescribed. Mother said she was not worried about a possible stroke. She was fragile in body but strong in faith. The Lord did grant Mother recovery from the surgery but not to her prior strength.

My heart was full of thanks for extra days with her. Another prayer was answered. Looking in on Mother at night I would voice a prayer that she felt loved. After the surgery, Mother softened in her disposition, was kinder, more gracious. All who were around her noticed the change in her personality. Even the night of Mother passing to her heavenly home, she was loving sharing God's love with all who came into her presence.

She was in the hospital but not critically ill as she usually was. One minute she was happily chatting with the physician's assistant who told her to get her lipstick on because her favorite doctor was right behind her. The next minute Mother asked my sister to raise her head higher but suddenly, quietly slipped away with a smile on her face from this earthly home to join loved ones in heaven.

Thanks

Always be joyful. Pray continually
And give thanks whatever happens.
That is what God wants for you in Christ Jesus.
1 Thessalonians 5:16-18 NCV

Be anxious for nothing, but in everything
by prayer and supplication
With thanksgiving, let your requests be made
known to God.
Philippians 4:6 NKJV

It is good to give thanks to the LORD, and to
sing praises to Your name, O Most High;
to declare Your loving kindness in the morning,
and Your faithfulness every night.
Psalm 107:1 NKJV

A Grateful Heart

Thank you, Lord,

….. for your promises to guide me, strengthen me, and direct my path through caregiving.
….. for the time that you gave me with my loved one. Through good and bad times, you were always there.
….. for forgiving my complaining when I was weary and stressed. Your Word tells us in Philippians 2:14 NLV to,

"Do everything without complaining."

….. for allowing me to share memories with Mother before you welcomed her to your home.
….. for giving her long life and a love for her family and friends.
….. for her mother's love.
….. for awakening my heart to all Your promises and making me the beneficiary of Your blessings.

Your Caregiving Daughter,

Meditate on My God's Creations

I Will Praise You,
Oh LORD,
With My Whole Heart.
I Will Tell of All Your Marvelous Works.

Psalm 9:1 NKJV

Conclusion

Thank you for reading *A Promise Kept, Spiritual Insights for Family Caregivers*. My hope is that these scriptures will give you God's peace, hope, and encouragement for any caregiving situation. They comforted me when I needed supernatural strength for each day.

I share lessons learned in my caregiving season with others to inspire them that though the road is not always smooth, it is worth the trip. God will guide you if you trust and believe He will.

Caregivers have many unique circumstances yet all have the responsibility to care for themselves physically, mentally, emotionally and spiritually. It is important to stay motivated and encouraged each day in order to give your best care.

Scriptures bring order into your life. Find scriptures that speak to you, strengthen you, and comfort you. Make them your own by turning them into declarations. Begin the day with them; during the day, speak them aloud to the LORD as,

> "LORD, you said to depend on you for help and I am asking for help. I thank you for help in _____."

Prayer at bedtime encourages peace and rest. Reflect on things that you are thankful for that God did for you during the day. Cast your concerns on him to give you rest and sleep without worry.

Refresh Your Heart: The 5 R's for Caregivers

"Caregivers need refreshing in mind and body as much as the loved one receiving care."

Rest: Get enough sleep, healthy food and exercise.

Realize: You do need help and support of others, accept it.

Restore: Restore your mind and spirit fifteen minutes daily with meditation, prayer or quietly enjoying nature.

Recognize: There are local agencies which provide information and/or assistance in caring for your loved one.

Remember: Family is a blessing; share their memories and create a legacy of love.

About the Author

Bonita planned to write educational articles and perhaps a children's book when she retired but plans changed when she became a full-time caregiver for her mother. This role impacted her life in so many ways. Her writing became documentary as she journaled medical notes and many to-do lists. Bonita also penned some stories as told to her by her mother about growing up during the Depression.

After her mother's passing she found a new purpose in writing and began writing articles and books in the caregiving genre. Bonita enjoys speaking to support groups, seniors, and the public to educate and bring awareness to caregiving issues.

One of her great joys is coordinating and hosting once a year during November, National Family Caregivers Month an event to recognize and celebrate family caregivers in her community.

Responding to questions from her audiences desiring information about how to share their stories in writing, Bonita created seminars in cooperation with the local library to encourage aspiring authors in self-publishing. Bonita loves motivating others to fulfill their dreams and find success in whatever roles they fill.

Bonita's Books

Do you know someone who is a caregiver? If so, please share one of my caregiving books with them. As a caregiver, I was too busy to shop but would have appreciated a book of encouragement. I know family caregivers will thank you.

A Promise Kept Spiritual Insights for Family Caregivers

A Promise Kept Inspirational Guide for Family Caregivers

Reflections, A Promise Kept Journal

Recipes That Warm the Heart, A Promise Kept Cookbook

A Caregiver Tip A Day, Reframing Your Story

A Guide to Self-Publishing When Your Dream is Becoming An Author

Books are available at Amazon, other online bookstores and by request signed copies from the author by contacting her email:

www.bbandariesAPROMISEKEPT@comcast.net.

www.ingramcontent.com/pod-product-compliance
Ingram Content Group UK Ltd.
Pitfield, Milton Keynes, MK11 3LW, UK
UKHW022217230426
12048UKWH00016BA/896